Deadliest Diseases of All Time

Ebola

Petra Miller

Cavendish
Square
New York

Published in 2016 by Cavendish Square Publishing, LLC
243 5th Avenue, Suite 136, New York, NY 10016

Library of Congress Cataloging-in-Publication Data

Miller, Petra, author.
Ebola / Petra Miller.
pages cm. — (Deadliest diseases of all time)
Includes bibliographical references and index.
ISBN 978-1-50260-652-5 (hardcover) ISBN 978-1-50260-653-2 (ebook)
1. Ebola virus disease—Juvenile literature. 2. Hemorrhagic diseases—Juvenile literature.
3. Epidemics—Juvenile literature. I. Title. II. Series: Deadliest diseases of all time.
RC140.5.M55 2016
616.9'1—dc23
2015008858

Editorial Director: David McNamara
Editor: Fletcher Doyle
Copy Editor: Cynthia Roby
Art Director: Jeffrey Talbot
Senior Designer: Amy Greenan
Senior Production Manager: Jennifer Ryder-Talbot
Production Editor: Renni Johnson
Photo Researcher: J8 Media

The photographs in this book are used by permission and through the courtesy of: Kenzo Tribouillard/AFP/Getty Images, cover
(inset); Studio_3321/Shutterstock.com, cover (background used throughout); Nati Harnik/AP Images, 4; WSBTV Atlanta/AP
Images, 6; Tom Washington/Moment Open/Getty Images, 8; Joel G. Breman, M.D., D.T.P.H./CDC, 11; jaddingt/Shutterstock.
com, 13; Jes Aznar/AFP/Getty Images, 17; Joe Raedle/Getty Images, 18; Dr. Lyle Conrad/CDC, 22; AP Photo/Timothy Jacobsen,
25; Tyler Hicks/Liaison/Hulton Archive/Getty Images, 26; Photodynamic/Shutterstock.com, 29; Michel du Cille/The Washington
Post/Getty Images, 32; filo/Digital Vision Vectors/Getty Images, 35; Nati Harnik/AP Images, 37; Chris Keane/Getty Images, 41;
Jane Hahn/Washington Post/Getty Images, 42; J Hindman/Shutterstock.com, 45; Dominique Faget/AFP/Getty Images, 48; John
Moore/Getty Images, 55; David Goldman/AP Images, 50.

Printed in the United States of America

Contents

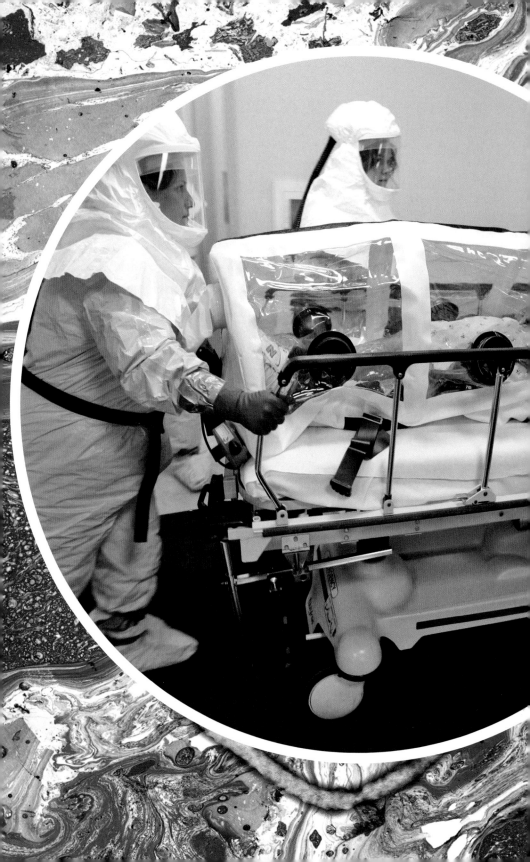

Introduction

People across the United States looked on in fear as television crews filmed Dr. Kent Brantly's walk from an ambulance into Atlanta's Emory University Hospital. Brantly had been in the West African country of Liberia. There he treated people with the deadly viral **hemorrhagic** fever, which is caused by an Ebola **virus**. The doctor was one of the two American aid volunteers who contracted the disease, and the first person known to bring the virus back to the United States. He had been flown home in a special plane in August 2014, and then driven by ambulance to the waiting hospital. Brantly was dressed in a full-body protective suit. This prevented him from **transmitting** the virus to others.

The airplane's isolation unit is equipped to carry only one patient at a time. After transporting Brantly to Dobbins Air Reserve Base, the plane returned to Liberia to pick up the virus's second victim, Nancy Writebol.

The fear people experienced was understandable. Ebola is a horrible and deadly disease, killing up to 90 percent of those who become infected. The first symptom might be a slight headache followed by a

Medical personnel at the biocontainment unit in Nebraska are trained to handle patients arriving with diseases such as Ebola.

Dr. Kent Brantly steps out of the ambulance that carried him to Emory University Hospital.

sudden high fever. Fatigue, diarrhea, and stomach pain quickly set in. Within less than a week's time the sickness thins the linings of the body's blood vessels and internal organs. Blood leaks into the intestinal tract and lungs. It seeps from the fragile surfaces of the gums. The victim suffers intense nausea and vomits a bloody, black liquid. The illness moves the body toward a state of general hemorrhage, or uncontrollable bleeding. This results in nosebleeds, bloodshot eyes, and sometimes even bleeding through the skin's pores. This is why it is called a hemorrhagic fever. Victims, most weakened from fluid loss, go into shock and die within days or weeks.

Ebola is an **emerging virus**. This means it is appearing in a population for the first time, or it has shown up before but is rapidly increasing in its incidence or range. The massive **outbreak** that struck in 2013 and was still active early in 2015 is the first ever to reach West Africa. The other outbreaks were restricted to Central Africa.

Ebola also is still somewhat of a mystery to scientists. Its source has not been positively identified, although it is believed that the virus begins in bats. Also, there is no approved cure for it or **vaccination** against it. The only treatment is what Dr. Bruce Ribner of Emory Hospital called "supportive care." In supportive care, doctors track a patient's symptoms, vital signs, and organ function. They supply fluids, electrolytes, and food. Treatments, such as blood transfusions and dialysis to keep patients stable while the patient's body fights the disease, are used.

"We just have to keep the patient alive long enough in order for the body to control this infection," Ribner said during an interview with Cable News Network.

Both Brantly and Writebol survived their infections, which were contained because both were held in isolation until they recovered. The infection is spread through contact with the bodily fluids of an infected person or with items contaminated by an infected person. The staff at Emory Hospital made sure this did not happen.

Unfortunately, Ebola victims in Africa do not have access to such great hospitals. This is one of the factors behind history's largest outbreak one of the world's deadliest diseases.

one Mystery Virus

There is no way of knowing how long the Ebola virus has been in existence, but we do know that it has only recently appeared in humans. It is a member of the virus family Filoviridae, which was first seen by scientists in 1967. That strain is called the Marburg virus because it infected laboratory workers in Marburg, Germany.

The virus was carried by a shipment of green monkeys brought to both Germany and the city of Belgrade (then Yugoslavia) for research and vaccine production. Thirty-one workers became infected, and seven died. The monkeys were euthanized to prevent the spread of the disease.

Ebola is the second **filovirus** to have been identified. Dr. Peter Piot, a microbiologist from Belgium, and his coworkers made the discovery. In 1976, Piot received a blood sample from researchers in Kinshasa, the capital of the central African nation of the Democratic Republic

Green monkeys carried the first filovirus into Europe, where it was identified.

of Congo (DRC), then known as Zaire. The blood had been taken from a Belgian nun who was an aid worker at a mission hospital in the small Congo village of Yambuku. She had died from an unknown disease.

Scientists in Zaire could not identify the virus in the blood. Using a commercial airliner, they transported it to Piot in Belgium with the question: "Yellow Fever?" When Piot put a sample under an electron microscope, he saw something he didn't expect. He thought it might be the Marburg virus, and sent the sample to the Centers for Disease Control and Prevention (CDC) in Atlanta, Georgia. There it was confirmed as a new virus.

Piot and his team then flew to the Congo, arriving in Africa not knowing what the disease was or how it was spread. He said in an interview in 2014 that the experience was frightening because they had no idea what they had to do to keep from getting the disease.

The Disease Hunters

The mystery disease intrigued virologists around the world. In Kinshasa, Piot met with the CDC's Karl Johnson and France's Pierre Sureau. Together, the three men flew to Yambuku. At the Yambuku hospital, they found buildings wrapped in long strips of gauze. The sisters had sealed the hospital to warn people of the danger of contagion. One of them, Sister Marcella, accompanied Piot and Sureau on a trip to the outlying villages.

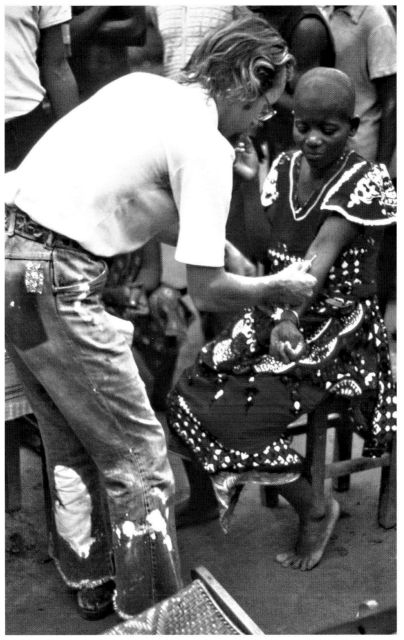

A member of an Ebola survey team collects a blood sample in
Yambuku in 1976.

En route, Piot and Sureau were impressed by the systems the people in and around Yambuku had created to halt the spread of the disease. They had installed blocks in the road, buried bodies in public cemeteries, and slowed or ceased traffic in the villages. The doctors realized that the worst of the **epidemic** had passed, largely due to the sensible way the local people had contained it.

The scientists set to work helping patients and collecting their samples. Carefully outfitted in goggles, rubber gloves, and surgical masks, they began entering the homes of infected villagers and taking blood samples. Occasionally, other scientists arrived to offer assistance, and medical supplies were delivered.

After some investigation, it was discovered that many of the dead had been pregnant women who had visited the Yambuku Mission Hospital for a vaccination. The first Ebola outbreak started at that hospital in August of 1976. The virus was traced to a forty-four-year-old mission worker, Mabalo Lokela. He had been traveling for two weeks. His wife, Sophie, who was eight months pregnant, had stayed at home. Four days later, on August 26, Mabalo came down with a sudden fever. Assuming he had a touch of malaria, he visited the hospital for a quinine injection.

Piot said there were only five needles and syringes at the clinic, and they were reused without being sterilized. Any needle that was used on Mabalo could then infect others with the Ebola virus. This is how so

Don't Touch

There are five strains or subspecies of the Ebola virus. Four can affect humans: Zaire ebolavirus (EBOV), Bundibugyo ebolavirus (BDBV), Sudan ebolavirus (SUDV), and Taï Forest ebolavirus (TAFV). Reston ebolavirus (RESTV) has caused illness in some animals but has not sickened any humans.

Ebola is a highly infectious disease but it is only mildly contagious. What makes the disease so infectious is that a small amount can develop into a fatal illness. However, it is passed from human to human only through direct contact with the infection. The most contagious diseases are ones that spread easily. They are usually airborne illnesses, such as measles or influenza. People can spread them through coughing or sneezing. An airline passenger with the flu, for example, can infect everyone on the flight.

The Ebola virus

many pregnant women died. There were other victims: people with malaria and children getting vaccinations against other diseases. The disease, Ebola hemorrhagic fever, spread to fifty-five villages, and was named after the Ebola River, which is nearby.

Medical facilities were closed because so many staff members had died, including several nuns who served at the Yambuku mission. This prevented the disease from being spread further by the use of unsterilized needles and the lack of what is known as barrier-nursing techniques. These techniques involve covering the caregiver's body so it never comes in contact with the body of the victim.

This and the actions of the villagers prevented widespread infection. But this didn't happen until 318 people had fallen ill with Ebola, and 280 of them had died.

As the scientists labored in Yambuku, rumors of a similar outbreak in Sudan began to spread. A virus expert at the World Health Organization (WHO) suggested that the Yambuku disease might match a mystery disease that had previously broken out in the tiny towns of Maridi and Nzara in southern Sudan. The expert, Paul Brès, wanted to compare the Yambuku samples with those of Maridi. Knowing this, a CDC scientist named Joseph McCormick drove his Land Rover 400 miles (644 kilometers) to Nzara. By the time McCormick crossed the Sudanese border and reached Nzara, the outbreak was slowing. McCormick spoke with patients and residents, and collected blood samples. He drove back to Yambuku, where the epidemic was also slowing.

Just before leaving Africa, McCormick announced that the outbreaks in Yambuku and Nzara were both Ebola. However, they were totally unrelated.

McCormick was convinced that no infected human being could possibly travel from Yambuku to Nzara in time to infect someone else. His Land Rover had been the first motorized vehicle on those roads in months. He had not found a single case of hemorrhagic fever in the towns between Yambuku and Nzara. Many of those towns had not even heard rumors of either outbreak, which means that each had a different source.

A Closer History

1967 The Marberg Virus is first identified in Marberg, Germany. Of the thirty-one victims, seven succumb to the emerging disease.

August 1976 Mabalo Lokela contracts the Ebola virus in the Congo village of Yambuku. He infects others in the local mission hospital before he dies. The disease spreads to 318 people, and 280 die.

September 1979 A newer, smaller outbreak of the Ebola virus spreads in the Sudan, in the city of Nzara. There are thirty-four cases and twenty-two deaths.

November 1989 Nearly 30 percent of an animal shipment to a US warehouse contracts another strain of the Ebola virus: Ebola-Reston—named for the Virginia city in which it was discovered. All are destroyed to contain the spread of the disease; no humans become ill.

May 1995 Ebola reemerges in the southwestern Congo, this time in the town of Kikwit. It claims 254 lives.

October 2000 Ebola tops 400 cases for the first time in an outbreak in the Gulu district of Uganda. There are 425 human cases and 224 deaths.

A form of the Ebola virus was found in pigs in the Philippines in 2008.

November 2008 The Ebola-Reston virus (RESTV) is detected in five workers on a pig farm and slaughterhouse in the Philippines. They suffer no symptoms. This is the first time the Reston virus has been found in pigs.

December 26, 2013 An outbreak begins in the Forest Region of Guinea and spreads to Liberia and Sierra Leone. There are more than twenty thousand cases and nearly eight thousand deaths by the end of 2014.

August 26, 2014 The Democratic Republic of the Congo suffers its seventh outbreak since 1976. A total of sixty-six cases and forty-nine deaths were recorded.

September 29, 2014 US troops arrive in Liberia to begin building hospitals to treat Ebola patients.

two Tracking Ebola

There have been ten cases of Ebola in the United States. The most infamous involved Thomas Eric Duncan. His was the first case, and he's one of only two Ebola patients in this country who died.

Duncan was a forty-two-year-old living in Monrovia, the capital of Liberia. There he rented a room from a family friend. In 2014, the friend's daughter became ill. Duncan helped her to a nearby hospital, but they were turned away because there was no room. The two returned home, where within a few hours, the daughter died. She had Ebola.

Duncan had already quit his job with a Liberian shipping company because he had a visa allowing him to visit the United States. Before boarding his September 19 flight, he was screened for fever. He showed no symptoms of Ebola. This is not surprising because the disease has an incubation period that

Workers carefully clean the apartment in Dallas where Ebola victim Thomas Eric Duncan stayed in 2014.

usually lasts eight to ten days. It can, however, last anywhere from two to twenty-one days. The incubation period is the time it takes for symptoms to begin after the virus enters the body.

Duncan's flight made stops in Brussels, Belgium, and Washington, DC, before landing in Dallas on September 20. Four days later he began showing symptoms. On September 25, he went to Texas Health Presbyterian Hospital. He told hospital staff that he was from West Africa, where the largest Ebola outbreak in history was raging. No one passed on the information. He was diagnosed with a mild fever and sent home but returned three days later when his condition worsened. On September 30, he tested positive for Ebola. Immediately the search was on for anyone else he might have infected. Texas health workers identified ten people, including the four who lived in the apartment where Duncan stayed. The people were removed from the apartment, which was then thoroughly cleaned.

Duncan was placed in isolation after he was admitted on September 28. On October 4, he was administered an experimental drug called brincidofovir. His kidneys failed. Duncan died in Dallas on October 8, 2014.

In the case of a viral disease, virus particles multiply in the victim's body. People become ill when they come in contact with the blood or bodily fluids of those who have the disease because that person's bodily fluids are full of live virus. For the **index cases**—the first victims of each epidemic—there are no earlier victims. Scientists assume that the index cases contract the virus from an animal that is sick or is a carrier. A carrier, or **vector**, animal is capable of carrying a virus in its own body without getting sick. When it comes in contact with another animal, such as a monkey or a human being that does not suffer from the disease, it infects them with the virus. This is one way that the Ebola virus spreads.

Anyone who contracts Ebola would be considered its "**host**." The place where a disease lives—such as in rats or tropical mosquitoes or coastal swamp water—is called its "natural **reservoir**." Usually, the reservoir occurs naturally in nature, **cycling**, or alternating between epidemics.

In the 1970s, no one had identified Ebola's natural reservoir. Also unknown was the vector animal. When Joseph McCormick said that the first outbreaks of Ebola, in Sudan and in the Congo, were unrelated, his conclusion was that they started with different vector animals.

The factory worker who was the index case in Nzara had most likely been exposed to a zoological reservoir (the rodents or insects in the cotton factory). Researchers believed Ebola must have stemmed from the cloth room. This theory seemed to narrow the search. Still, the cloth room contained a jungle of life forms. It housed bats, rats, spiders, cotton boll weevils,

A 1976 Ebola outbreak in Sudan was traced to this factory in Nzara.

and thousands—if not millions—of insects. The researchers began collecting vast numbers of specimens and sent them to the CDC for testing. All specimens were tested—the results came back negative. Not one of the creatures living in the cloth room was a reservoir for Ebola. But McCormick kept thinking of the bats.

Return to Nzara

In September of 1979, the WHO contacted McCormick, who was then head of the CDC's Special Pathogens Branch (including viruses). They needed his help with a new outbreak in Nzara, Sudan. It looked like Ebola. The outbreak had begun in August and spread quickly. Local doctors had quarantined the area, but there was no guarantee of containment. McCormick remembered the southern Sudanese landscape. He knew how much work it would take to comb the ten-foot grasses of the Sudan savanna for hidden villages and unidentified cases of Ebola.

When McCormick arrived in Khartown, Sudan, he found himself facing fear over the outbreak and a gasoline shortage. No one wanted to travel to Nzara and the cost of the trip was astronomical. McCormick finally persuaded a pilot to take him. The pilot agreed only to drop McCormick at the landing strip. McCormick insisted he wait for blood samples. That way, the pilot could fly them back, and McCormick could get quick lab results. The pilot was reluctant, but McCormick bribed him to stay in his closed plane until dawn.

After landing, McCormick headed straight to the hut that housed twenty Ebola patients. Each had fevers of more than 105 degrees Fahrenheit (40.5 degrees Celsius). Their joints and muscles ached, and their throats were too sore to swallow. Many were disoriented and some were too sensitive to bear the touch of clothes against their skin. McCormick had little equipment and almost no protective gear. He wore only one pair of latex gloves and a respirator to keep him from breathing in contaminants. He examined the victims, jotting down their particular symptoms and taking blood samples. McCormick then packed his samples with dry ice and ran back to the runway, where he secured the package and sent the pilot back to Khartoum. He then expanded his work.

McCormick tested people, sequestered people, and ministered to them through his protective garb. He provided respirators, gloves, and surgical clothing to everyone who attended the funeral of an Ebola victim. Within a month, the outbreak was contained.

The Monkey Tragedy

The fact that one infected animal can set off an epidemic hit CDC and American Army scientists with the force of a bomb in 1989. A group of monkeys in Reston, Virginia, ten miles west of Washington, DC, began dying of what looked like Ebola. The site of the outbreak was a Hazleton Research Products warehouse. Hazleton imported and sold laboratory animals.

On October 4, 1989, one hundred wild, crab-eating macaques from the Philippines arrived at the Hazleton warehouse. By November 1, twenty-nine of the hundred monkeys had died. Veterinarian Dan Dalgard dissected one of the dead monkeys to see if he could figure out the cause of death. He took a sample of monkey mucus to the nearby United States Army Medical Research Institute of Infectious Diseases (USAMRIID). There, it was discovered that the monkey was a victim of a filovirus. The idea that a filovirus might burn through a warehouse ten miles from the capital of the United States greatly concerned

Biosafety pressure suits are used at the US Army Medical Research Institute of Infectious Diseases at Fort Detrick.

the Army scientists. Their first task was to identify the virus. Tests showed that the Reston monkeys had Ebola-Zaire.

To prevent any possibility of infection in the human population, the monkeys were painlessly put to death and the facility was cleaned. Meanwhile, two of four monkey caretakers at the facility were hospitalized. One had a heart condition, the other a high fever and nausea. Both men survived their illnesses unharmed. It is hard to guess why Ebola-Reston caused the violent hemorrhagic death in the monkeys and not in humans. Probably, a very tiny difference in the genetic code of the virus caused it to react in a completely different way.

Nurse Babu Washington Stanley at St. Mary's Hospital in Uganda contracted Ebola in 2000 and survived.

Ebola Returns

In the spring of 1995, Ebola returned to southwestern Congo in the town of Kikwit. By May 12, the death toll was forty-eight of sixty-five cases. According to the head of virology at Kinshasa University, this number was about to rise. Researchers could not identify the index case, but the first-known patient was a thirty-six-year-old man named Kimfumu. He fell ill in early May with a fever and distinct red-and-blue skin discoloration.

Kimfumu worked as a Kikwit hospital laboratory assistant. In fact, nearly two-thirds of the victims were hospital workers. The outbreak, which included the neighboring towns of Mosango and Yasa Bongo, was potentially far more serious than the 1976 Yambuku outbreak. Kikwit, with a population of 400,000, was a more dangerous site for a major epidemic than an isolated village such as Yambuku.

As the death toll rose, so did international attention and aid. Doctors and researchers arrived from WHO and the Red Cross. They brought with them rubber boots, plastic slippers, gloves, goggles, surgical masks, and full-length robes. They tried explaining to the people of Kikwit the dangers of traditional burial rituals, in which women cleaned dead bodies by hand. Red Cross teams drove into the bush around Kikwit. Using battery-powered loudspeakers, they called out the precautions people needed to take. Their voices were heard.

Roadblocks were set up to keep people out of Kinshasa and away from the capital city's five million residents. On June 2, the WHO announced that the outbreak was completely halted. Like every previous Ebola outbreak, the disease surged seemingly from nowhere, killed swiftly, and burned itself out. The final death toll was declared: of the 315 people who became ill, Ebola had killed 254.

Outbreak Grows

There was another Ebola outbreak in October of 2000, this time in the northern Gulu district of Uganda. The

Non-Human Victims

In late September 1999, ecologist J. Michael Fay began a trek across 1,200 miles (1,931 km) of central African wilderness. He called the journey "Megatransect." His goal was to collect as much data as possible about the area's forests, fields, and swamps. The trip was both grueling and fruitful.

In June of 2000, Fay walked into the Minkébé forest, which is located in northeastern Gabon and covers more than 12,500 square miles (32,375 sq km). The Minkébé is one of the last massive wilderness areas in central Africa.

While in the Minkébé, Fay observed the low number of gorillas. For weeks, he neither saw nor heard the animal and found only one pile of gorilla dung. In the same amount of time on similar terrain in Congo, he might have found four hundred piles. It occurred to him that an Ebola epidemic might have burned through the gorilla population.

This observation coincided with those of the Minkébé forest rangers. They too had found a bizarre lack of gorillas and chimpanzees in the Minkébé. By comparison, the 1984 findings

Ebola may be responsible for the disappearance of gorilla populations in some regions of Africa.

of two researchers placed the gorilla population of the Minkébé at 4,171. A population of 4,000 gorillas would certainly have been visible to an ecologist with Fay's observational skills.

scrub savanna of the Gulu district is quite different from the wetter, richer rain forest of Congo. Although less vicious than some of the other outbreaks, this epidemic was larger—the first one with more than four hundred cases. There were 425 people infected between October and the epidemic's official end on February 27, 2001. The death toll was 224.

At first, the epidemic seemed more like a fever. The early cases lacked the explosive hemorrhaging that characterized the Yambuku outbreak. Then, one night, Simon Ajok, a thirty-two-year-old nurse, stormed down the hall of St. Mary's Hospital. He was hemorrhaging from his nose, gums, and eyes. His bloody coughs smeared the white walls with lethal fluids. Simon had contracted Ebola while caring for patients in the hospital's isolation ward.

The hospital staff imposed anti-infectious measures such as the use of protective gloves, clothing, and facial masks. Then they called Dr. Matthew Lukwiya. The St. Mary's outbreak was confirmed as Ebola.

The Ugandan Health Ministry alerted the WHO and the CDC. These agencies sent local people into the towns and villages to warn others, explain preventive measures, and to find any other sufferers. As a result, the number of Ebola patients at St. Mary's began to rise. Lukwiya attempted to contain the outbreak. He kept victims in strict isolation at the hospital and from their families—despite not knowing how the disease traveled.

Lukwiya's hard work saved hundreds or possibly thousands of lives. His handling of the Uganda epidemic has also provided the CDC virologists, for the first time, blood samples from Ebola victims at every stage of infection. Unfortunately, Lukwiya himself contracted the virus. He was the last health-care worker to die of Ebola during Uganda's 2000 epidemic.

There have been twenty-four Ebola outbreaks, and most of the cases since 2000 have begun with hunters handling infected primates. There have been several on the border of the Congo and Gabon. The first, in 2001–2002, began when six people became infected by touching dead gorillas, chimpanzees, and antelopes. The disease was then spread, causing 124 cases and 97 deaths. None of the outbreaks was as deadly as the one in Uganda, although there was a big one in 2007 in Bamoukamba, Congo. In this case, a person became ill after buying an infected bat. The disease spread to nearby villages, sickening 264 people and killing 187.

What is common to all of the outbreaks except one is their location: they all occurred in a belt from Uganda in the east to Gabon in the west of central Africa. When Ebola finally moved, it caught authorities by surprise and the outbreak was bigger than all the others combined.

three Seeking a Cure

E bola is a part of a group of viruses known as the filoviruses. A filovirus is a negative-stranded **RNA** virus. Its genome, or basic form, is a single strand of ribonucleic acid (RNA). RNA, like deoxyribonucleic acid, or **DNA**, contains genetic information.

Viruses are not independent life forms, meaning they cannot multiply on their own. A virus needs a host cell in which to **replicate**. Thus a virus is actually a parasite that, once it invades a living cell, can reproduce. In order to reproduce, a living creature passes on its genetic information to its offspring. This genetic information is contained within the body's DNA and RNA material.

Double-stranded DNA is the blueprint for an entire organism, such as an ant or a badger, or a human being. It exists in every one of the millions of cells in a human or animal and contains all of the

In September of 2014, steady streams of Ebola patients overwhelmed the workers at Redemption Hospital in Monrovia, Liberia.

information about the creature to which it belongs. DNA uses RNA to make more of the correct type of DNA for any given organism. However, in an RNA virus, there is no DNA blueprint. It would be impossible for an RNA virus to reproduce, or replicate itself, without invading a host cell and taking over that host's copy-making machinery. In short, once a person contracts Ebola, his or her body naturally contains all that is needed for the virus particles to quickly multiply.

The outside of a filovirus is made up of seven proteins. At least one is able to shut down a victim's immune system, much the way Human Immunodeficiency Virus (HIV) does. However, it moves at a much faster pace than HIV. When the virus genome gets inside a host cell, it makes a copy of itself. It uses this copy to create new, identical negative genomes. This is how a virus develops.

When the virus has made as many particles as it can, the host cell is so swollen with large blocks or "bricks" of virus particles that it dies and "bursts." This bursting action releases the new pieces of virus into the body. They attack healthy host cells and widen the circle of infection. As the copies attack other host cells, more of the cells are turned into virus factories.

The virus also makes proteins. One of them blocks immune cells from calling in antibodies that could keep an infection from spreading. The Ebola virus moves quickly through the bloodstream, affecting collagen, which keeps your organs in place. It focuses

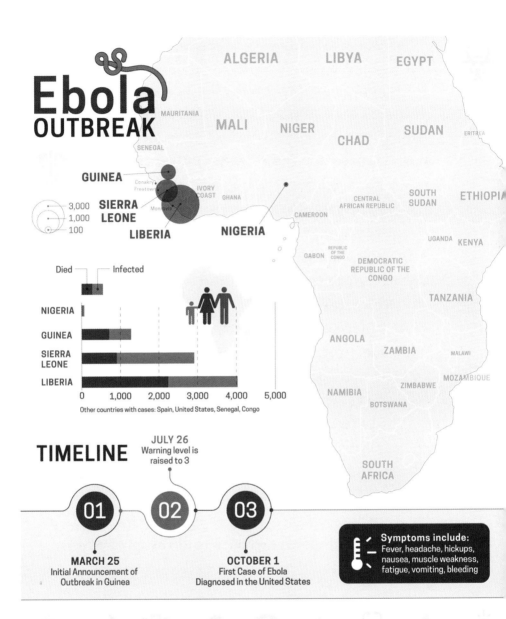

Ebola OUTBREAK

GUINEA

- 3,000
- 1,000
- 100

SIERRA LEONE

LIBERIA

NIGERIA

Died ──── Infected

- NIGERIA
- GUINEA
- SIERRA LEONE
- LIBERIA

| 0 | 1,000 | 2,000 | 3,000 | 4,000 | 5,000 |

Other countries with cases: Spain, United States, Senegal, Congo

TIMELINE

01

02

JULY 26
Warning level is
raised to 3

03

MARCH 25
Initial Announcement of
Outbreak in Guinea

OCTOBER 1
First Case of Ebola
Diagnosed in the United States

Symptoms include:
Fever, headache, hickups,
nausea, muscle weakness,
fatigue, vomiting, bleeding

This graphic shows how rapidly the Ebola virus spread in West
Africa from the time it was first reported until it finally reached the
United States.

Back to the Front Lines

Doctor Richard Sacra was the third American health-care volunteer to be infected with the Ebola virus in Africa and brought back to the United States for treatment. He was diagnosed on September 1, 2014 while working in Monrovia, Liberia, and quickly flown to a facility in Omaha, Nebraska, where he was placed in isolation.

Sacra was given the drug TKM-Ebola. He also received blood donated by Dr. Brantly, who flew to Nebraska after it was discovered his blood was a perfect match for Sacra's.

Debbie Sacra, the doctor's wife, said during a news conference: "It really meant a lot to us that he was willing to give that donation so soon after his own recovery."

The WHO said in September that using blood from a survivor was highly experimental but it was worth trying. Whether Sacra fully recovered is unknown—he was released from isolation after three weeks. He continued his lengthy rehabilitation at home in Massachusetts. This period included a trip back to the hospital when it appeared that he might have relapsed.

Sacra is a missionary doctor working for a group called Serving In Mission (SIM). He returned to Liberia when his

Dr. Richard Sacra spent three weeks in isolation at the Nebraska Medical Center and survived an Ebola infection.

health improved in January 2015. He will treat patients suffering from illnesses such as malaria and diabetes, as well as those in maternity and pediatrics wards. He will not treat Ebola patients.

"I think about those in Liberia who have survived Ebola and are having to deal with all these same kinds of challenges with so much less help than what I've had," Sacra said during a news conference in Omaha, Nebraska. "The experts tell me I'm immune. I don't plan to test that, but I'm grateful for it."

on organs and tissue, such as the liver, lymph nodes, kidneys, ovaries, and testes. It does not affect the bones. The destruction of these tissues leads to bleeding in the mucus membranes, abdomen, and genitals. As the viral colonies grow, they make tiny holes in the organs and tissues they have occupied. This leads to hemorrhagic bleeding from the eyes, ears, nose, mouth, and sometimes directly from the pores of the skin. When the blood leaks, less of it gets to the body's organs. This reduces the amount of oxygen the organs receive, which causes the organs to begin to shut down.

Ebola is a horrible disease, and doctors began searching for a cure as soon as it was identified. Peter Piot collected **antiserum** from people who survived the first outbreak in 1976 in Yambuku. An antiserum is a serum containing antibodies against a specific disease. On his second trip to Sudan, Joseph McCormick was stuck by a needle while taking a blood sample from a woman believed to have Ebola. Thinking he had only a few days of health left, he injected himself with the antiserum collected by Piot.

When two other doctors arrived, they began a trial of the Yambuku plasma. They injected patients with the same antiserum McCormick had used on himself. Some of the patients seemed to respond positively. Others did not. Ultimately, there was no definite evidence either way. It turned out that McCormick didn't need the antiserum. The woman he was treating when he suffered the needle prick did not have Ebola.

The most powerful medical weapon against a virus has been a vaccine. Composed of "killed" or weakened virus, a vaccine is either injected or taken orally. It introduces just enough of a disease into a person's body to stimulate the production of antibodies— the immune system's weapon against a disease— without causing a person to fall ill. Ebola is so deadly that the use of actual virus particles seemed too dangerous. As with much radical medical research, the first step has been to create a vaccine for animals.

New Developments

A research team at the National Institutes of Health (NIH) developed an Ebola vaccine for monkeys. Nancy Sullivan, Anthony Sanchez, Pierre E. Rollin, Zhi-yong Yang, and Gary J. Nabel first injected guinea pigs with a DNA immunization against a rodent version of Ebola. This stimulated an immune response in the animals' cells. Researchers then increased the animals' immune response. They did this with a weakened version of a common cold virus. The virus was scientifically altered to express Ebola virus proteins. This means that without using actual Ebola, researchers were able to force the guinea pigs' bodies to increase its defenses against Ebola proteins.

After the successful tests on guinea pigs, the team focused on monkeys. The vaccine was a success. The vaccinated monkeys did not get sick. The others died within days. This is an important first step, but it is not the same as a human vaccine. There are numerous differences between the infection of a monkey in a lab and falling ill during an epidemic from contact with the fluids of an Ebola victim.

In the early 2000s, scientists from Canada and the United States announced that they had created a vaccine that protected monkeys from Ebola in every instance. According to the *New York Times*, trials on people were scheduled to begin within two years, and be finished by 2010 or 2011. However, the expense of these trials was great and there was little demand for a vaccine at that time. The trials then were never started.

Thomas W. Geisbert, who helped develop the vaccine, said: "It takes a crisis sometimes to get people talking [and say] 'OK. We've got to do something here.'"

Another Ebola crisis arrived in West Africa in 2013. Scientists are now working hard to find drugs than can cure the disease. Funding for research is also increasing.

While at Emory University, Dr. Brantly and Nancy Writebol were given the drug ZMapp, which is based on engineered antibodies. The medication seemed to play a role in their full recovery. Funding from the US Defense Threat Reduction Agency will allow Mapp Biopharmaceutical to conduct more early-stage clinical trials on the drug.

Nancy Writebol received an experimental drug while being treated for Ebola at Emory University Hospital.

The Food and Drug Administration gave TKM-Ebola, the drug given to Dr. Richard Sacra in Nebraska, a fast-track designation to speed testing.

There is also a push to find vaccines against Ebola. The WHO announced that clinical trials for two vaccines are under way. Health-care workers in affected countries will be given the first chance to use the experimental vaccines.

four Starting Small

The first person to die from Ebola in West Africa was not a hunter, a hospital caregiver, or a factory worker. The victim was a two-year-old boy, Emile Ouamouno. The toddler lived in the village of Meliandou, located in a southern Guinea rain forest. Researchers refer to Emile as "patient zero."

According to the WHO, "In Africa, infection has been documented through the handling of infected chimpanzees, gorillas, fruit bats, monkeys, forest antelope and porcupines." However, no one knows how this young boy became infected. On December 2, 2013, Emile had a fever, black stool, and was vomiting. He died four days later.

By January 1, 2014, his mother, his three-year-old sister, and his grandmother had also died. From there the infection spread: from people who attended the grandmother's funeral to a midwife to a health-care worker who treated the midwife to a doctor at a hospital miles away where the health-care worker had gone for treatment.

Three sisters of patient zero Emile Ouamouno play outside their home in Meliandou, Guinea.

Bat Out of Hell

The Ebola virus starts in animals and moves on to humans. Viruses need a carrier, or vector, animal capable of carrying the virus without becoming ill. Vector animals can infect many other animals and humans. The Human Immunodeficiency Virus (HIV) was carried by monkeys and passed on to humans. The Ebola virus kills monkeys and apes as well as humans, so it needs another carrier.

Scientists believe the fruit bat is the most likely natural reservoir. Infected fruit bats can carry the virus across rivers and other borders—the virus doesn't appear to affect them. The bats can infect fruit when they gnaw on it, and the virus can be passed on to animals that then eat that fruit. Scientists also believe all twenty-four known Ebola outbreaks were started when a human touched the blood or the meat of an infected ape, monkey, antelope, or bat killed in the bush for food. This is one way that the Ebola virus spreads.

The fruit bat is a delicacy in Guinea and other countries in West Africa. It is served either dried or in a soup. Cooking the meat at a high temperature will kill the virus, but anyone who handles an animal before it is

Ebola

The fruit bat can carry the Ebola virus without being infected.

cooked is in danger of getting the disease. The fruit
bat is known to live in the rain forests of Guinea,
and it is the suspected source of the outbreak in
West Africa.

Meliandou lost fourteen residents in the four months after Emile died and is now free of Ebola. The disease, however, spread from Guinea to Sierra Leone and Liberia.

For viruses to spread rapidly they need an accelerator or an event to speed the process. In HIV, the accelerator was an unsanitary facility that produced plasma. A lot of HIV-tainted plasma was sent to the United States, where it infected many hemophiliacs and others who required blood transfusions. In West Africa, there were several accelerators. One was a lack of trained medical people. Another was an absence of proper isolation facilities. A third was the arrival of Ebola in large population centers.

One grave mistake made in Guinea was that hospitals and public health services let more than two and a half months pass before informing the Ministry of Health and *Médecins sans Frontières* (MSF or Doctors Without Borders) about clusters of the disease. This gave Ebola too much time to spread.

Sixty field workers from MSF arrived in Guinea in late March of 2014 to try to stop the outbreak. By that time the country had already reported 112 Ebola cases and 70 deaths. Senegal closed its border with Guinea on March 29, and MSF reported the spread of the epidemic as "unprecedented."

When the virus reached Conakry, the capital city of Guinea, it went "viral" in the words of an American doctor. By mid-June, the disease was found in sixty locations in Guinea, Liberia, and Sierra Leone. This made it difficult to isolate the virus.

Threats to health-care workers—already in short supply in the affected countries—complicated matters. Liberia, for example, had fewer than 250 physicians for more than four million residents. In one instance, rural Guinea residents attacked MSF clinics because they thought foreigners brought the disease. In another, youths attacked an isolation clinic in Liberia. There was hostility toward outsiders, who were driven from affected villages.

The threat extended beyond physical violence. The WHO reported in January 2015 that in Guinea, Liberia, and Sierra Leone there were 825 health-care workers infected. Of these, a reported 493 had died. In some places, clinics closed due to a shortage of medical personnel.

Dr. Jerry Brown is the medical director of a Christian mission hospital on the outskirts of Monrovia, the capital city of Liberia. He is one of the "Ebola Fighters" who combined, were named Person of the Year by *Time* magazine for 2014. He told *Time* magazine that people easily traveled from rural areas to Monrovia for work, and they could easily transport Ebola into the city of 750,000 residents. When the disease showed up in rural Liberia in March, Brown admitted, "we really started panicking."

That panic was not shared by the country's health officials, who did not immediately respond. Work was left to people like Brown. He and his staff first researched Ebola. They then made the decision to convert the mission's chapel into an isolation unit, where the first

Protected workers at a hospital run by Doctors Without Borders bring in a possible Ebola patient for treatment

Ebola patients were brought for treatment. One had died in the ambulance, and the other died days later. Ambulance personnel arrived wearing ordinary scrubs. A nurse from the ambulance was infected, as was the first doctor to examine the patients.

The disease spread quickly, and clinics were soon overwhelmed. Dr. Brantly was infected at Dr. Brown's clinic. Schools in Liberia were shut down to prevent further spread of the disease. One elementary school was turned into an Ebola clinic, a decision that angered residents. Many were leery about sending children to the school when classes resumed. They did not trust the government to clean the school properly.

It wasn't until August of 2014, that many international health organizations acknowledged Ebola as a disaster. The United States responded by sending marines to Liberia. President Barack Obama announced that the United States would help the governments and health-care systems in Liberia, Sierra Leone, and Guinea by training thousands of health-care workers and building treatment centers. The World Bank donated $400 million to fight the disease.

The work done by the United States and other countries slowed the spread of Ebola, but the disease was still devastating West African countries in early 2015. The WHO reported on January 16, 2015, that there had been twenty-one thousand cases in the outbreak in eight countries and more than 8,468 deaths.

Among the devastating changes brought on by Ebola is the number of orphans it creates. Often, family members who fear getting the virus reject those children. One of the heroes of Sierra Leone was Augustine Baker, who worked at a home for Ebola orphans. He would go into neighborhoods seeking these children. The orphanage had helped about two hundred children in the first year of the outbreak before tragedy struck. Baker contracted the disease himself and died in late February of 2015.

Despite gains in the fight against the outbreak, it was far from over.

five Developing Defenses

When Thomas Eric Duncan died in Dallas on October 8, 2014, the Ebola virus lived on. Two nurses at Texas Health Presbyterian Hospital were infected. They are the only people infected with the disease in the United States.

Amber Joy Vinson was diagnosed with the virus on October 15, and was immediately flown to Emory University Hospital in Atlanta. There she received plasma from both Brantly and Nancy Writebol. She spent less than two weeks in isolation before doctors announced that she was free of the virus. Another nurse who treated Duncan, Nina Pham, was treated for Ebola at the National Institutes of Health Clinical Center in Bethesda, Maryland. She also survived.

Vinson and Pham are the only people to have acquired Ebola while they were in the United States. The country has taken steps to make sure that no one else gets infected. In October 2014, the CDC stated

Nurse Amber Vinson had a joyful departure from Emory University Hospital.

that anyone arriving from one of the countries hard hit by Ebola would be monitored for twenty-one days. This is the incubation period for the disease.

Additionally, all flights from Liberia, Guinea, and Sierra Leone would have to land at one of five airports: John F. Kennedy in New York, Newark Liberty Airport in New Jersey, Washington Dulles International Airport, Hartsfield-Jackson Atlanta International Airport, or O'Hare International Airport in Chicago.

"We're announcing a new system that will further protect Americans from Ebola," CDC director Thomas Frieden said. "The bottom line here is we have to keep up our guard against Ebola. These additional steps will protect families, communities and health-care workers."

One of the steps is to screen all incoming passengers from affected countries. This process involves taking a person's temperature—fever is one of the first symptoms of Ebola. The CDC also asked that flight attendants ask any ill passengers if they have been in West Africa in the previous twenty-one days. If the answer is yes, and the passenger is exhibiting Ebola symptoms, attendants are to use hand hygiene and other infection control measures. Other passengers on the flight are not in danger because Ebola is not an airborne disease. They can only get the disease from touching bodily fluids from an infected person.

Also, it is illegal to bring bushmeat, or wild meat, into the United States. Bushmeat is the source of the Ebola virus in some countries. All wild meat in the United States is safe to eat.

The United States was fortunate that Duncan didn't infect more people. All four patients treated at Emory University Hospital survived. Dr. Bruce S. Ribner, who oversaw their care, admitted that a lot was learned while treating the patients. Among the lessons was that even if a patient needed dialysis or ventilator support, it was not too late to save that person.

"I think we have shown our colleagues in the United States and elsewhere that that [being too late] is certainly not the case, and therefore, I think we have changed the algorithm for how aggressive we are going to be willing to be in caring for patients with Ebola virus disease," he said during a *New York Times* interview.

What the world has learned about fighting Ebola is that any outbreak needs to be addressed quickly. Progress was not made in slowing the spread of the disease in West Africa until patients could be isolated and treated, and safe burial practices were accomplished. For example, in August 2014, the sick were refused treatment because with only 350 beds in Ebola centers, there was no place to put them. By mid-December there were two thousand beds and not enough patients to fill them. At the height of the epidemic, Liberia reported three hundred new cases each week. By January 2015, the country had only twelve confirmed cases.

Infections remained widespread in Sierra Leone, where there are only two nurses for every ten thousand people. However, infections in the region didn't come close to the 1.4 million predicted by the CDC. It appears the infection is being contained. This is really good news, but it does present a problem. The WHO's Martin Friede, coordinator of the group's drug development, told NPR that it's hard to conduct drug trials when there are few patients. "On the one hand, the number of Ebola cases has really dropped dramatically … This is excellent for the countries involved," Friede said during an interview. "However, from a drug research and development perspective, this is not so good."

Chimerix halted one of its two drug trials on patients in Liberia in early 2015. The company explained the termination by stating that only a handful of people had signed up to participate in the trial.

Bacteria can be dangerous to humans (causing such diseases as cholera and tuberculosis) or they can be beneficial (living in the human digestive tract). They can be killed by medications called antibiotics (anti meaning "against" and biotic meaning "bacteria"). Viruses are never beneficial. They are also very difficult to destroy. Drug companies are trying to find ways to do this.

Vaccines are given to healthy people to keep them from ever getting ill. Work on Ebola vaccines is going strong. In a first clinical trial of an experimental vaccine conducted by researchers at the National Institutes of Health, twenty volunteers developed anti-Ebola antibodies within four weeks of injection. All of those tested tolerated the vaccine well.

A volunteer receives an injection during a 2015 Ebola vaccine study at Redemption Hospital in Liberia.

Two vaccines, including the one tested by the NIH, will enter Phase II and III trials. These trials are scheduled to be conducted on twenty-seven thousand healthy volunteers in Liberia. Results are expected by June 2016. Other research is being done on a vaccine in pill form, which would make it easier to administer and to store.

Trials on vaccines in Liberia can still be productive even if there are no Ebola patients around. Blood tests can measure the immune response to a vaccine in humans. If the response is similar to the one in monkeys (the vaccine has proven to protect them), the vaccine can be approved.

Ebola is a security concern for the United States in a small way. There are reports that some countries and terrorist groups have tried to grow the virus to use in biological warfare. The Japanese terrorist group Aum Shinrikyo (the group responsible for releasing sarin gas in a Tokyo subway in 1995) sent a medical team to Africa during a 1992 outbreak to collect some of the virus. The team failed in its efforts. However, the *Scientific American* reported that handling the disease poses a greater threat to the terrorists than to anyone they might target.

The greatest threat posed by Ebola is that it appears in countries that are poor, often politically unstable, and lack a health-care system sufficient enough to stop an outbreak on its own. The epidemic in West Africa proves what can happen when governments and international health organizations are slow to respond to an appearance of the disease. Perhaps when the next outbreak occurs, the world will be ready.

Glossary

antiserum Extract from the blood of a person (or animal) who suffered or is immune to a particular disease and therefore carries the antibodies that fight that disease.

cycling A virus existing in nature in natural reservoirs, remaining infectious though inactive while waiting for a host.

DNA A nucleic acid that carries the genetic information in a cell and is capable of self-replication and synthesis of RNA; the sequence of the nucleotides in the two strands of DNA determines hereditary characteristics.

emerging virus A virus that has jumped species or geographical areas due to genetic mutation or to changes in external conditions such as those caused by human patterns of expansion and development.

epidemic An outbreak of a contagious disease that spreads rapidly and widely.

filovirus A virus type that includes Ebola and Marburg; characterized by a long wormlike shape with a curled end.

Glossary

hemorrhagic Characterized by excessive bleeding. Ebola hemorrhagic fever is caused by an infection with the Ebola virus.

host The organism (like a human being) in which another organism (like a parasite or virus) lives or replicates.

index case The first patient to come down with a disease during an outbreak; of interest because tracing the cause of the index case's infection explains the origin of the outbreak.

outbreak A sudden eruption of cases of a given disease.

replicate The way genetic material makes an exact copy of itself.

reservoir An organism or population that transmits a pathogen (like a virus) while being immune to its effects.

RNA A chain of phosphate and ribose units whose structure is crucial to the communication of genetic information.

transmitting To communicate an infection from one organism to another.

vaccination A medical treatment, administered by injection or orally, that protects a patient against a particular disease.

vector An organism or species that carries disease-causing microorganisms from one host to another.

virus An ultramicroscopic infectious agent that replicates only within the cells of living hosts; many are dangerous to their hosts.

For More Information

2014 Ebola Outbreak in West Africa

www.cdc.gov/vhf/ebola/outbreaks/2014-west-africa/

The Centers for Disease Control and Prevention provides and overview and updates on the largest Ebola outbreak in history.

Ebola Virus Disease

www.who.int/mediacentre/factsheets/fs103/en/

The World Health Organization's information and fact sheet page contains sections on the transmission, identification, prevention, and treatment of Ebola, as well as background on the disease.

Ebola Virus Infection

www.webmd.com/a-to-z-guides/ebola-fever-virus-infection

WebMD details the symptoms, treatment, and prevention of Ebola, a posts links to the latest news about the deadly virus.

Interested in learning more about Ebola?
Check out these websites and organizations.

Organizations

Centers for Disease Control (CDC)
1600 Clifton Road
Atlanta, GA 30333
(800) 311-3435
(404) 639-3311
www.cdc.gov

United States Army Medical Research Institute of
Infectious Diseases
USAMRIID
1425 Porter Street
Fort Detrick
Frederick, MD 21702
www.usamriid.army.mil

World Health Organization (WHO)
525 23rd Street NW
Washington, DC 20037
(202) 974-3000
www.who.int

For Further Reading

Books

Chapnick, Dr. Edward K. *Ebola Myths & Facts for Dummies*. Hoboken, NJ: For Dummies, 2015.

Garrett, Laurie. Ebola: *Story of an Outbreak*. New York: Hatchette Books, 2014.

Piot, Peter. *No Time to Lose: A Lifetime in Pursuit of Deadly Viruses*. New York: W.W. Norton and Company, 2012.

Preston, Richard. *The Hot Zone: A Terrifying True Story*. New York: Random House, 1994.

Quammen, David. *Ebola: The Natural and Human History of a Deadly Virus*. New York: W.W. Norton and Company, 2014.

Quammen, David. *Spillover: Animal Infections and the Next Human Pandemic*. New York: W.W. Norton and Company, 2012.

Zimmer, Carl. *A Planet of Viruses*. Chicago: University of Chicago Press, 2012.

Index

Index